Rwanda

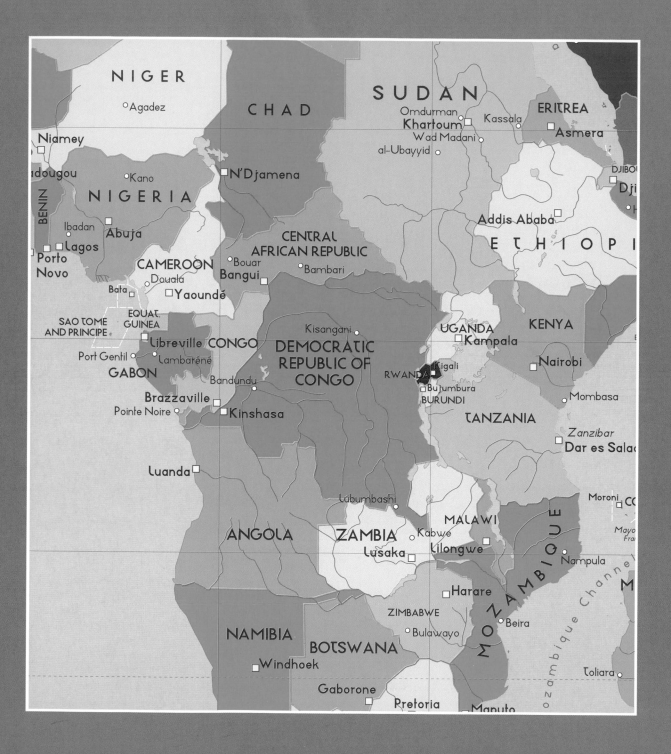

RWANDA

Andy Koopmans

Mason Crest Publishers
Philadelphia

Produced by OTTN Publishing, Stockton, N.J.

Mason Crest Publishers
370 Reed Road
Broomall, PA 19008
www.masoncrest.com

3 5 7 9 8 6 4 2

Library of Congress Cataloging-in-Publication Data

Koopmans, Andy.
  Rwanda / Andy Koopmans.
     p. cm. — (Africa)
  Includes bibliographical references (p.   ) and index.
  ISBN 1-59084-812-8
  1. Rwanda—Juvenile literature. I. Title. II. Series.
  DT450.14.K66 2004
  967.571—dc22

                                    2004004826

Table of Contents

Africa: Continent in the Balance
Robert I. Rotberg

Africa is the cradle of humankind, but for millennia it was off the familiar, beaten path of global commerce and discovery. Its many peoples therefore developed largely apart from the diffusion of modern knowledge and the spread of technological innovation until the 17th through 19th centuries. With the coming to Africa of the book, the wheel, the hoe, and the modern rifle and cannon, foreigners also brought the vastly destructive transatlantic slave trade, oppression, discrimination, and onerous colonial rule. Emerging from that crucible of European rule, Africans created nationalistic movements and then claimed their numerous national independences in the 1960s. The result is the world's largest continental assembly of new countries.

There are 53 members of the African Union, a regional political grouping, and 48 of those nations lie south of the Sahara. Fifteen of them, including mighty Ethiopia, are landlocked, making international trade and economic growth that much more arduous and expensive. Access to navigable rivers is limited, natural harbors are few, soils are poor and thin, several countries largely consist of miles and miles of sand, and tropical diseases have sapped the strength and productivity of innumerable millions. Being landlocked, having few resources (although countries along Africa's west coast have tapped into deep offshore petroleum and gas reservoirs), and being beset by malaria, tuberculosis, schistosomiasis, AIDS, and many other maladies has kept much of Africa poor for centuries.

Thirty-two of the world's poorest 44 countries are African. Hunger is common. So is rapid deforestation and desertification. Unemployment rates are often over 50 percent, for jobs are few—even in agriculture. Where Africa once

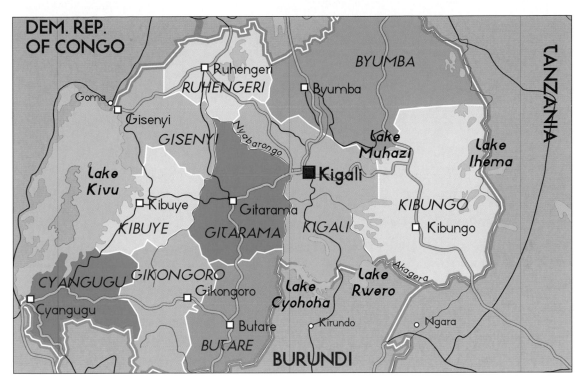

A landlocked country, Rwanda features the magnificent Lake Kivu.

was a land of small villages and a few large cities, with almost everyone engaged in growing grain or root crops or grazing cattle, camels, sheep, and goats, today more than half of all the more than 750 million Africans, especially those who live south of the Sahara, reside in towns and cities. Traditional agriculture hardly pays, and a number of countries in Africa—particularly the smaller and more fragile ones—can no longer feed themselves.

There is not one Africa, for the continent is full of contradictions and variety. Of the 675 million people living south of the Sahara, at least 130 million live in Nigeria, 67 million in Ethiopia, 55 million in the Democratic Republic of the Congo, and 45 million in South Africa. By contrast, tiny Djibouti and Equatorial Guinea have fewer than 1 million people each, and prosperous

A Hutu woman carries a basketful of vegetables near Gotovo, Rwanda.

Botswana and Namibia each are under 2 million in population. Within some countries, even medium-sized ones like Zambia (11 million), there are a plethora of distinct ethnic groups speaking separate languages. Zambia, typical with its multitude of competing entities, has 70 such peoples, roughly broken down into four language and cultural zones. Three of those languages jostle with English for primacy.

Given the kaleidoscopic quality of African culture and deep-grained poverty, it is no wonder that Africa has developed economically and politically less rapidly than other regions. Since independence from colonial rule, weak governance has also plagued Africa and contributed significantly to the widespread poverty of its peoples. Only Botswana and offshore Mauritius have been governed democratically without interruption since independence. Both are among Africa's wealthiest countries, too, thanks to the steady application of good governance.

Aside from those two nations, and South Africa, Africa has been a continent of coups since 1960, with massive and oil-rich Nigeria suffering incessant periods of harsh, corrupt, autocratic military rule. Nearly every other country on or around the continent, small and large, has been plagued by similar bouts of instability and dictatorial rule. In the 1970s and 1980s Idi Amin ruled Uganda capriciously and Jean-Bedel Bokassa proclaimed himself emperor of the Central African Republic. Macias Nguema of Equatorial Guinea was another in that same mold. More recently Daniel arap Moi held Kenya in thrall and Robert Mugabe has imposed himself on once-prosperous Zimbabwe. In both of those cases, as in the case of Gnassingbe Eyadema in Togo and the late Mobutu Sese Seko in Congo, these presidents stole wildly and drove entire peoples and their nations into penury. Corruption is common in Africa, and so are a weak rule-of-law framework, misplaced development, high expenditures on soldiers and low expenditures on health and education, and a widespread (but not universal) refusal on the part of leaders to work well for their followers and citizens.

Conflict between groups within countries has also been common in Africa. More than 12 million Africans have been killed in the civil wars of Africa since 1990, with more than 3 million losing their lives in Congo and more than 2 million in the Sudan. War between north and south has been constant in the Sudan since 1981. In 2003 there were serious ongoing hostilities in northeastern Congo, Burundi, Angola, Liberia, Guinea, Ivory Coast, the Central African Republic, and Guinea-Bissau, and a coup (later reversed) in São Tomé and Príncipe.

Despite such dangers, despotism, and decay, Africa is improving. Botswana and Mauritius, now joined by South Africa, Senegal, Kenya, and Ghana, are beacons of democratic growth and enlightened rule. Uganda and Senegal are taking the lead in combating and reducing the spread of AIDS, and others are following. There are serious signs of the kinds of progressive economic policy changes that might lead to prosperity for more of Africa's peoples. The trajectory in Africa is positive.

(Opposite) The lush green area around Lake Kivu, in the western region of Rwanda, supports numerous types of plant and animal life. (Right) Lake Kivu is the largest body of water in Rwanda and the highest lake in Africa.

1 Land of a Thousand Hills

COVERING ONLY 10,169 square miles (26,338 square kilometers), Rwanda is one of the smallest nations in Africa, yet that small area contains a great variety of natural wonders. This central Africa country, which shares borders with Burundi, the Democratic Republic of the Congo, Tanzania, and Uganda, has white-capped volcanic mountains, lush forests, deep valleys, grassy *savanna*, and numerous lakes and rivers.

Rwanda is also one of Africa's highest countries, with most of its terrain lying at elevations greater than 5,000 feet (1,525 meters) above sea level. Varying elevations help determine Rwanda's geographical regions, which include the Great Rift Valley along the western border; the Virunga Mountains in the northwest; the Congo-Nile Divide on the eastern edge of the Great Rift Valley; the central plateau; and the lowlands of the east.

Great Rift Valley

Rwanda sits on the eastern edge of a branch of the Great Rift Valley, an enormous fissure that cuts north to south through the continent. The valley was formed when the African and Eurasian *tectonic* plates separated around 35 million years ago. The portion of the valley lying within Rwanda's borders is a strip of land running between Lake Kivu and the Congo-Nile Divide.

Lake Kivu lies on the Great Rift Valley's western branch. It is a freshwater lake and Rwanda's largest body of water, with a surface area of 1,042 square miles (2,699 sq km). The border between Rwanda and the Democratic Republic of the Congo (DRC) runs through the lake, dividing it roughly in half between the countries.

Once part of a larger body of water that filled a section of the Great Rift Valley, Lake Kivu was formed by volcanic lava deposits along the northern shore. It is the highest lake in Africa, at 4,787 feet (1,459 meters) above sea level, and boasts beautiful beaches, a rough, jagged coast, and an archipelago of islands. It is the only navigable body of water in the country, but its limited depths only allow for shallow-draft barges and native craft.

The land surrounding the lake is a rich habitat for wildlife that includes eucalyptus, acacia, oil palms, elephants, hippopotamuses, crocodiles, wild boars, leopards, antelopes, and flying lemurs. Although the lake contains 32 species of fish, there is little flora in the water due to great volumes of poisonous *methane* gas rising from beneath the lake. The shores of Lake Kivu also boast important archeological sites where the oldest stone tools in the world have been found.

Quick Facts: The Geography of Rwanda

Location: Central Africa, east of Democratic Republic of the Congo
Area: (slightly smaller than Maryland)
  total: 10,166 square miles (26,338 sq km)
  land: 9,630 square miles (24,948 sq km)
  water: 536 square miles (1,390 sq km)
Borders: Burundi, 180 miles (290 km); Democratic Republic of the Congo, 135 miles (217 km); Tanzania, 135 miles (217 km); Uganda, 105 miles (169 km)
Climate: temperate; two rainy seasons (February to April, November to January); mild in mountains with frost and snow possible
Terrain: mostly grassy uplands and hills; relief is mountainous with altitude declining from west to east
Elevation extremes:
  lowest point: Rusizi River, 3,117 feet (950 meters)
  highest point: Volcan Kirisimbi, 14,826 feet (4,519 meters)
Natural hazards: periodic droughts; the volcanic Virunga Mountains are in the northwest along the border with Democratic Republic of the Congo

Source: CIA World Factbook, 2003.

Congo-Nile Divide

The Virunga Mountains, located in the northwest region and marking part of the Rwanda-Uganda border, are a chain of extinct volcanoes running along the northern edge of the Congo-Nile Divide. They encompass Volcanoes National Park, which covers more than 48 square miles (125 sq km) and has eight volcanoes. Five of the volcanoes—Sabyinyo, Gahinga, Bisoke, Muhabura, and Karisimbi—lie within Rwanda's borders.

At 14,787 feet (4,507 meters) high, Karisimbi is the loftiest point in Rwanda (it is slightly higher than Mount Whitney, the tallest mountain in the

Rwanda's Volcanoes National Park, located in the Virunga Mountains, is home to about half of the world's remaining population of wild mountain gorillas.

continental United States). Karisimbi has the shape of a huge dome, its width covering a large section of the mountain range. In Kinyarwanda, the language of Rwanda, *Karisimbi* means "white shell," a reference to the volcano's often white-capped summit.

Karisimbi Volcano contains four belts of vegetation. The belt of bamboo forest serves as one prominent habitat for mountain gorillas, for which Volcanoes National Park is home. Some mountain gorillas stand as high as 6 feet and weigh more than 400 pounds (181 kilograms). These animals are gentle, timid vegetarians and live in extended families. Once numbering in the tens of thousands, only hundreds now exist in the wild, and approximately 600—about half the world's population—survive in this region of Rwanda. The famed mountain gorilla researcher Dian Fossey conducted most of her observations in the area around Mount Karisimbi.

From the eastern side of the Great Rift Valley, a chain of dramatically ridged mountains rises to form the western slopes of the Congo-Nile Divide (also known as the Congo-Nile Crest). The peaks of the divide average an altitude of 9,000 feet (2,743 meters), and some summits along the range reach 10,000 feet (3,048 meters).

The Congo-Nile Divide is so named because it acts as a *watershed* for Africa's two great river systems: the Congo and the Nile. From the divide the Nile River flows north to the Mediterranean Sea and the Congo flows west to the Atlantic Ocean. In the lower elevations of the western slopes, land clearing and periodic flooding have caused severe soil erosion.

The higher elevations of the Congo-Nile Divide hold most of Rwanda's remaining forests, which include the Gishwati and Nyungwe Forests. These forests and the Virunga Mountains together make up the Albertine Rift Mountains Ecoregion, which encompasses sections of Rwanda and four other countries. It is one of the world's most plentiful and diverse faunal regions.

The Nyungwe Forest contains the spring that is the source of the River Nile. It is also the habitat of 13 recorded primate species—25 percent of the primates of Africa—as well as 300 species of birds, 200 species of trees, and more than 100 species of orchids.

Plateau and Lowlands

Lying to the east of the Congo-Nile Divide, at an elevation ranging between 4,000 and 6,000 feet (1,219 and 1,828 meters), lies Rwanda's central plateau. It is an expanse of countless mountains and valleys and is the inspiration for the county's nickname, "Land of a Thousand Hills."

One particular problem in the plateau region is *deforestation*. Prior to the 20th century, almost 30 percent of Rwanda's land was covered in great forests; however, by the end of the century less than 7 percent remained. Deforestation, along with over-farming and cattle grazing, is responsible for the serious soil erosion and depletion that the lands of the central plateaus have suffered. Over the past decades, the government has combated soil problems by building hedges and dikes throughout the region. Also, Rwandans have introduced terrace farming, a method of growing crops that adapts to the terrain of hills.

East of the central plateau, the terrain slopes into the grassy savanna and swamps of the country's lowlands. This area, which ranges in elevation between 3,280 and 4,920 feet (1,000 and 1,500 meters), is lush and green in the rainy seasons and brown and dry in the dry seasons. Soil erosion and fires during the dry seasons have destroyed much of the savanna.

Most of the country's 23 lakes are located in the lower eastern portion of Rwanda, where elevations drop to 3,000–4,000 feet (915–1,220 meters). The eastern region also contains Akagera National Park, named for the Akagera (or Kagera) River. This waterway, which constitutes much of the eastern border with Tanzania, is the largest *tributary* of Lake Victoria.

Created in 1934, the Akagera National Park covers 965 square miles (2,500 sq km) and its diverse wildlife attracts many visitors. The park contains buffalo and zebras, antelope and warthogs, chimpanzees and lions, as well as elephants, rhinoceroses, hippopotamuses, and rare animal species like the giant anteater. The park was once one of the most beautiful and best maintained in Africa, but heavy poaching reduced its wildlife considerably during the 1990 civil war and the 1994 genocide, when people in hiding desperately hunted for food. However, it still is home to a remarkable selection of birdlife, with over 500 species living along the Akagera.

Climate and Seasons

Although Rwanda lies near the equator, its high altitude makes the temperature mild rather than hot. The average daytime temperature is between 86°F and 93°F (30°C and 34°C), but in the highlands it can fall between 53°F and 59°F (12°C and 15°C). On the country's mountaintops it can drop below freezing. The mountains also receive 71 inches (180 centimeters) of rain each year, while the lowlands may only get as little as 31 inches (80 cm) annually.

Rwanda has four seasons: a short dry season in January and February; a rainy season from March to May; a longer dry season from June to September; and another rainy season from October to December. The country also experiences occasional *droughts*, usually during the dry seasons. These droughts are often severe, and because rainfall waters most of Rwanda's crops, they sometimes cause serious food shortages or even famine.

(Opposite) A Tutsi cattle herdsman tends to his duties on a farm near Butare. (Right) A Hutu man takes baskets to sell at a market near Ruhengeri. Traditionally farmers, the Hutu people use baskets like these while collecting their harvests.

2 A Tale of Tribes

PRIOR TO COLONIZATION, Rwanda's history was not written but passed down through a rich oral tradition of folklore that goes back a thousand years to the first human inhabitants of the region, the Twa. Members of the small-statured and dark-skinned African race known as the Pygmies, the Twa lived in the forests as hunter-gatherers. Archaeological findings suggest the Twa settled in the region as far back as 30,000 B.C. The group held sway over most of the country until the 11th century, when groups of Bantu-speaking farmers called the Hutu grew to power.

The Hutu had settled in Rwanda between the 7th and 10th century, and by the 1400s they had established small farming communities throughout most of the country. As increasing numbers of Hutus settled in Rwanda, they claimed more land on which the Twa had once hunted. To maintain their lifestyle without hindrance, many Twa moved into the higher forests.

The next group of inhabitants, the Tutsi, came to Rwanda between the 14th and 15th centuries. They were warriors and cattle herdsmen who migrated to the area from the African Nile River Basin in search of land their cattle could graze. The Hutu, the Tutsi, and the Twa lived together for centuries, sharing the same land and language and belonging to the same extended clans. Members from the different ethnic groups often intermarried and had children; however, families kept track of bloodlines and knew if they extended back in time to Tutsi, Hutu, or Twa.

Although they were far outnumbered by the Hutu, the Tutsi gradually gained dominance between the 15th and the 17th century. They did this primarily through their superior combat abilities and their possession of cattle, which in African tradition was equated with wealth and status. One of the Rwandan clans settled in the center of the region and developed a monarchy. While many of its leaders and rulers were Hutu, during the 1600s absolute power was conferred on one Tutsi king, called a *mwami*.

The mwami was believed to be divine and thus was treated like a god. According to the Tutsi legend of the mwami's origins, three heaven-born children—two brothers and their sister—accidentally fell to earth. They brought with them fire, the forge, iron, and cattle, elements that signify power and wealth. One of the brothers, Kigwa, married his sister, Nyampundu, and formed the first Tutsi clan. A descendant of this clan, Gilhanga, first led the Tutsi to the land that is present-day Rwanda. His son, Kanyaruanda, became the first mwami, and all subsequent mwamis trace their divine lineage to him.

From the 1600s to the 1800s, the Tutsi monarchy expanded throughout much of Rwanda, conquering lands that formerly belonged to the Hutu. The Tutsi eventually dominated the Hutu socially, economically, and politically, except in some remote border areas where a few Hutu chiefs remained defiant against the Tutsi monarchy and maintained their power.

The Tutsis maintained control over most of the Hutus through a *feudal* system called *ubuhake*. Under this system, Hutu serfs pledged themselves to Tutsi nobles by laboring in their fields, tending their cattle, and serving in armies. In exchange, the Tutsis granted Hutus the use of cattle and land protection from foreign enemies. (Some Tutsis who were not part of the aristocracy—also known as petit-Tutsis—entered into *ubuhake* with more powerful Tutsi lords; however, they did not perform labor but only served as soldiers.)

This was a profitable arrangement for the Tutsi lords; for the Hutus, it meant suffering economic and social oppression. As with the European system of feudalism, it was rare for a Hutu peasant to gain enough wealth to free himself from service to his lord. Further, the obligations of *ubuhake* were passed down from father to son, allowing the Tutsi aristocracy to subjugate the Hutu peasantry generation after generation. When the first Europeans arrived to Rwanda in the 19th century, this system was still in place.

The Europeans Arrive

Because Rwanda's high and mountainous terrain protected it from invaders and slave traders, Rwandans escaped the fate of slavery that befell many other Africans between the 17th and the 20th centuries. The terrain also impeded Europeans from exploring and colonizing Rwanda until the end of the 19th century.

The first Europeans to colonize Rwanda were the Germans, who under the rule of Otto von Bismarck sought to colonize Africa to develop international trade markets. During what is known as the Scramble for Africa, the German Empire (1871–1918) competed with other European nations—particularly the British Empire—to gain as much African territory as possible. In 1885, representative leaders of the world's superpowers met at the Berlin Conference to settle issues over African lands, including those not yet claimed. As part of the negotiations, Rwanda and its neighboring kingdom

German Otto von Bismarck (1815–98), the first chancellor of the German Empire, was one of the first Europeans to gain a foothold on international trade in Africa.

to the south, Burundi, were *annexed* as a single colony called German East Africa (or Rwanda-Burundi). This was nine years before the first European even set foot in Rwanda.

A German delegation led by Count Gustav Adolf von Götzen and Richard Kant arrived in Rwanda in 1894. When von Götzen and Kant met with the king, Mwami Kigeli IV Rwabugiri, and his Tutsi chiefs, they took note of the Tusti-Hutu power structure in place. They were impressed by the orderly coexistence of the three distinct ethnic groups, who lived side by side, spoke the same language, and even belonged to the same clans. This stood in contrast to many other colonized areas of Africa where clans and tribes constantly fought each other.

The Germans sought an efficient and effective way to rule Rwanda-Burundi. While in other African colonies Europeans ruled directly by manipulating or changing the social and political structure, the Germans sought to rule indirectly by taking advantage of the established order. Their timing proved excellent, because a year after the first German delegation arrived, the powerful Mwami Rwabugiri died and the monarchy was left in question. After some violent internal conflict within the family, one of the mwami's sons, Yuhi V Musinga, emerged as the successor. However, the situation was not stable and Musinga needed outside assistance. As a gesture of goodwill, the Germans pledged military support to the new king. With their advanced weapons and military techniques, the Germans helped Musinga bring the Hutu-ruled border areas under his control. In exchange, Musinga became Germany's military and political ally and a tool to establish power in Rwanda.

While the colonizers ruled indirectly and did not aim to change

Rwandan society, they did introduce some Western institutions to the new colony. Key among these was the creation of the country's first missions. They worked to convert Rwandans to Christianity and educate children using Western methods.

The Germans also made several economic changes to support the mass plantation of coffee and tea for export. As a result, many Rwandans were pressured to grow these *cash crops* rather than the crops that they needed for food. The colonizers also collected a cash tax, which meant that for the first time Rwandans had to trade their labor for money rather than goods or service.

The Germans continued to maintain and even expand on the *ubuhake* system. In helping Musinga enlarge his control over the border areas, the Germans enforced the Tutsi rule over the Hutus and extended the *ubuhake* system to those who greatly resented it.

Following Germany's defeat in World War I, Belgium gained control over the colony as a spoil of war, and for several years the country governed indirectly, as the Germans had done. In 1923 the League of Nations, an organization established by international treaty to settle disputes between countries, officially gave Belgium administrative control over Ruanda-Urundi. The mandate required Belgium to allow the existing political structure to remain in place; however, by 1925 Ruanda-Urundi had become an important piece of the Belgian colonial empire and a potential source of great wealth. The following decade, the Belgians implemented a series of reforms that dramatically changed the colony's social and political structure.

Mwami Musinga was not welcomed into this new structure. The Belgians did not trust the mwami because he had been a close ally of the

Germans, longstanding rivals in Africa. In 1931, the Belgians forced Musinga to abdicate his throne and go into exile in the southwestern part of the country. His son, who ruled under the name Mwami Rudahigwa Mutara III, was installed in his place, although his power was much diminished. The Belgians maintained the real political power, instituting a civil service bureaucracy that their own colonial administration controlled, and which was staffed almost exclusively by Tutsis.

In 1935, the Belgian administration issued identification cards to all Rwandans, which they were required to carry. The cards denoted whether they were Twa, Hutu, or Tutsi. Like the Germans before them, the Belgians gave preference to the Tutsi because they were Rwanda's de facto leaders. They also preferred the Tutsi for their appearance: while the Hutu were typically short and broad, the Tutsi were taller, thinner, and had features thought to be more Caucasian. The predominant belief in Europe at the time was that the white race was superior; thus, in the minds of many Belgians, the Tutsi's appearance made them genetically superior to the Hutu and the Twa.

Using this ethnic preference as its basis, the Belgian administration introduced *apartheid*, a system of segregation and preferential treatment that favored the Tutsis, even though they only made up approximately 15 percent of the population. The Belgians made sure the Tutsis had the best jobs and better educational opportunities. Under the system, many Tutsis naturally felt superior to the other ethnic groups; meanwhile, the Hutus' second-class position made many resentful. The animosity between the groups increased when in 1943 the Belgian administration replaced local chieftains—most of whom were Hutu—with Tutsi chiefs appointed by the mwami.

Hutu Revolution

Soon after it was established at the end of World War II, the United Nations changed the terms of Belgium's control over Rwanda-Burundi. The mandate would become a trust territory, to be prepared ultimately for independence. Rwandans would be granted political rights and would become more involved in the government. Belgium responded to the order by granting rights exclusively to the Tutsi.

Following World War II, colonies throughout Africa and the rest of the world began to agitate for independence. In Rwanda, the Hutu led the movement, demanding political representation equal to their numbers. In the late 1950s, the group began forming political parties, and in 1957, several Hutu intellectuals published a *manifesto* demanding better treatment and representation.

In 1959, the country erupted in violence as Hutus rose up and attacked Tutsis. The Belgians, who believed that they could retain their rule over the country for a longer period if they remained uninvolved, stood by during the fighting. Tens of thousands of Tutsis, including the king, fled to neighboring Uganda for safety, and the Tutsi kingdom fell.

Following the uprising, elections were held and the Hutu government replaced the Tutsi-dominated one. In 1961, Belgium recognized the new government as the Rwandan Republic. Then, in 1962, Rwanda and Burundi were redivided into separate countries. Prior to colonization, the two kingdoms had often been hostile toward each other, so the colonial union had been an uneasy one. The United Nations recognized the independence of both countries; the colonial rule of nearly 60 years had ended.

Gregoire Kayibanda, Rwanda's first president and a Hutu, led the government in establishing Hutu power over the Tutsi minority during the late 1950s and subsequent decades.

The Rwandan Republic

Rwanda's first president was Gregoire Kayibanda, one of the authors of the 1957 Hutu Manifesto. Although Rwanda was now an independent African state, Kayibanda's government maintained the racist hierarchy of power established by the Belgians. The only difference was that now Hutus were in control and the Tutsis were oppressed, often through violent means.

During the 1960s and 1970s, Tutsis who had fled to other countries organized and attempted several invasions to retake the government; however, these actions repeatedly failed and brought violent repercussions upon the Tutsis living in Rwanda. The worst of these reprisals occurred in December

1963, when over 20,000 Tutsis were massacred. Other outbreaks of violence against Tutsis occurred in 1967 and 1973. The violence caused yet more Tutsis to flee the country. Over the years, tens of thousands were exiled.

President Kayibanda was reelected in 1969, but he was overthrown four years later by Major General Juvenal Habyarimana, one of Kayibanda's own officials. Habyarimana dissolved the National Assembly, suspended the government's constitution, and ruled for many years as president-dictator. He established his own political party, Le Movement Revolutionaire National pour le Development (MRND), and outlawed all other political parties. For 27 years he ruled with little overt opposition.

Civil War

In 1990, civil war broke out in Rwanda when approximately 10,000 members of the Rwandan Patriotic Front (RPF), an army of exiled Tutsis trained in Uganda, invaded from the north. Many of these soldiers were children of Tutsis who had been exiled in the early 1960s. Unable to repel the well-trained invaders, President Habyarimana negotiated a cease-fire with the RPF in March 1991. The rebel group agreed to the cease-fire under the condition that the president would legalize other political parties in the country and allow elections to take place. Habyarimana acceded to the demand. On January 10, 1993, the government and opposition parties signed the Arusha Accords, an agreement that established a plan for a multiparty government in Rwanda. However, ethnic violence between Hutus and Tutsis broke out the next month, leaving hundreds of people on both sides dead. A new peace agreement was negotiated between the government and the RPF in August. To prevent further outbreaks, 2,500 United Nations peacekeeping troops were brought into the country in October 1993.

Despite the progress toward a new multiparty government, Hutu extremists did not want to share power with the Tutsis. These men—among them many government officials—planned a genocidal attack on the country's Tutsis and moderate Hutus. The preparations for the genocide included gathering and hiding weapons, training a militia, and broadcasting *propaganda* on the radio that encouraged hatred and using violence against the Tutsis. The attack against the Tutsis began on April 6, 1994, after President Habyarimana and Burundian president Cyprien Ntaryamira, a Hutu, were killed when their plane was shot down. (The plane's attackers are still unknown.) Within an hour of the assassinations, the Hutu militia attacked.

The violence began in the capital city of Kigali and spread within days all over the country. Extremist leaders convinced many Hutu citizens to take part in the mass killings. The violence was massive and horrific. Organized gangs roamed through the street killing every Tutsi they found, often hacking them to death with machetes. Neighbor killed neighbor, and in many cases Hutu men and women were forced to kill their Tutsi spouses. More than half the Hutu population took part in the slayings, including men, women, children, and the elderly.

Meanwhile, UN soldiers stationed in Rwanda were ordered not to respond. In fact, after 10 Belgian UN soldiers were killed in the violence, the UN pulled out 90 percent of its forces, leaving many Tutsis to die unprotected. The RPF rebel army ended the violence when it captured Kigali on July 4, 1994. Fearing Tutsi retribution, Hutu government officials fled into neighboring

Victims of the 1994 genocide killings are laid to rest at this gravesite, in an area outside Kigali where approximately 20,000 people died.

countries along with almost 2 million Hutus, creating an international refugee crisis. In Rwanda, the streets and rivers were filled with corpses. Within 100 days an estimated 800,000 Tutsis and moderate Hutus had been slaughtered.

A Temporary Peace

On July 17, 1994, the RPF created a new transitional government, which would remain in power until elections could be held. A moderate Hutu, Pasteur Bizimungu, was made president, and a transitional multiparty National Assembly was established in Kigali.

In late 1994, the Rwandan authorities began arresting genocide participants by the thousands. Within months, the prisons were overcrowded with more people than the justice system could handle. The first trials began in 1995. Meanwhile, the United Nations General Assembly voted to establish the International Criminal Tribunal for Rwanda (ICTR) for the purpose of prosecuting high-level leaders from the government, military, media, and church. The tribunal was set up in neighboring Tanzania in the city of Arusha, and was given a mandate to last until 2008.

At the end of 2003, in one of the most publicized ICTR trials, three high-level media officials charged with inciting genocidal violence were convicted and given lengthy prison sentences. However, due to a lack of resources and other difficulties, the tribunal has moved at a very slow pace. By early 2004 the ICTR had only completed the trials of 10 of the 66 arrested leaders.

Estimated Deaths and Refugees Resulting from Ethnic Violence in Rwanda

To date, Rwanda has seen its worst outbreaks of ethnic fighting in 1959 and 1994. These numbers represent the victims in those years and immediately following.

	1959	1994
Deaths	20,000	800,000
Refugees	150,000	2,000,000

Sources: bbc.co.uk; CIA World Factbook, 2003.

The Hutu-Tutsi conflict eventually extended beyond Rwanda's borders. In 1996, the new Rwandan government sent troops into Zaire (now the Democratic Republic of the Congo, or DRC) to attack Hutu refugee camps that they believed had become sites of military organizing. The Rwandan government claimed that many of the refugees were being held hostage by these forces. It wanted the refugee population to return to Rwanda to reintegrate into society and, when necessary, to face justice. It also wanted to remove the potential threat of an invasion by Hutu extremists.

In 1997, Rwandan forces joined with Zairean rebels to depose President Mobutu Sese Seko, who was supporting the Hutu extremists. When Sese

Rwandan president Paul Kagame (left) arrives with South African president Thabo Mbeki to a peace summit in 2003. Under Kagame, a new constitution was ratified to protect citizens' basic rights and help prevent another genocide.

Seko stepped down in 1998, Zaire was given its present name, and Laurent Kabila became president. However, Kabila refused to expel Hutu extremist militias from the country, so Rwanda again joined with opposition forces. Rwanda fought with the DRC until a peace agreement was signed in 2002, under which Rwanda promised to pull out troops and the DRC agreed to disarm Hutu militias within its borders. By October 2002, Rwanda claimed it had pulled out the last of its troops.

The New Government

President Bizimungu remained in office until April 2000, when he resigned over a dispute with his Cabinet. He was succeeded by Vice President Paul Kagame, a Tutsi and RPF leader. Under Kagame's leadership, village-based courts were established in 2001 to help prosecute genocide suspects. Additionally, the country introduced a new flag and national anthem in an attempt to forge unity.

In 2003, voters helped ratify a new constitution, and President Kagame was reelected president in the country's first elections since 1994. Also, Kagame's RPF party won a 95 percent absolute majority in the country's first multiparty parliamentary elections. Both elections enjoyed a large turnout, but European Union observes raised doubts about the presidential election, claiming that ballot box stuffing and voter intimidation had occurred at some polls. However, Kagame rejected the charges and the election results were made official.

(Opposite) The Chip Building, located across the street from the Rwandan Presidential Palace, hosts meetings between the government and the private sector. For security reasons, it is illegal to take photographs of the heavily guarded palace. (Right) Members of Parliament meet to discuss new laws here in the National Assembly building.

3 The New Republic

RWANDA IS AN INDEPENDENT, *sovereign*, democratic, secular state that holds to the principle of government of the people, by the people, and for the people. National sovereignty belongs to the citizens, who exercise it directly by way of *referendum* or through their representatives. All people aged 18 and older have the right to vote. In 2003, the Rwandan government adopted a new constitution designed to provide and protect basic human rights for all Rwandan citizens, to fight ethnic division, and to ensure against another genocide at the hands of the government.

Rwanda is divided into 12 administrative regions called prefectures, subdivided into 116 districts or municipalities. Prefectures are headed by prefects; districts and municipalities are administered by burgomasters or mayors. Like the U.S. government, upon which the 2003 constitution was based, Rwanda's central government is divided into three branches:

legislative, executive, and judicial. Each branch oversees the actions of the others with a system of checks and balances.

The Legislative Branch

The Rwandan legislature is represented by a *bicameral* Parliament. The two houses are the Chamber of Deputies and the Senate, led respectively by the speaker of the Chamber of Deputies and president of the Senate. The tasks of Parliament are to deliberate on and pass laws, to legislate, and to oversee the executive branch. It holds three sessions, each of two months' duration, every year.

There are 80 members in the Chamber of Deputies, elected for five-year terms. Fifty-three of the seats are elected through a national vote; the remaining members are elected by local and national special interest committees or appointed by political parties.

The Senate is composed of 26 members, at least 30 percent of whom must be women. (The quota system is responsible for Rwanda having the highest worldwide representation of women in its national government.) Members serve one non-renewable term of eight years. Twelve of the Senate members are elected by committees from each region of the country; eight are appointed by the president of the Republic; four are designated by the Forum of Political Organizations; and two are university lecturers. These specific quota requirements ensure that formerly underrepresented groups have a guaranteed voice in the government, and that any one political party does not gain excessive power. This latter concern was particularly important because Habyarimana's MRND-led government had ruled as a dictatorship.

The Executive Branch

The government's executive power is vested in the president and his or her cabinet. The president is the head of state and the guardian of the constitution. He or she guarantees national unity, government stability, and the country's independence, and enters into international agreements and addresses the nation whenever necessary.

A presidential candidate must be at least 35 years old, have been born in Rwanda, and have at least one parent of Rwandan origin. He or she is elected by national referendum to a term of seven years, renewable only once. The president has numerous powers. He or she may *promulgate* laws, call national referendums, mint money, approve members of the Cabinet, sign orders approved by the Cabinet, make appointments of senior government officials, and bestow *clemency*. The president is also commander-in-chief of the Rwanda Defense Forces and may declare war or states of emergency or siege. As a check on the executive power, declarations of war, emergency, or siege must be approved by Parliament. Finally, the president represents Rwanda in its foreign relations and may sign treaties, peace accords, and armistices.

The Cabinet is comprised of the prime minister, 17 ministers, and 11 lower-ranking ministers called Ministers of State, each appointed by the president. It implements national policy upon agreement of the president, deliberates upon bills and laws, and drafts executive orders. The prime minister is second in power to the president and coordinates the functioning of the Cabinet, including assigning duties and presiding over meetings.

Bills intended to become law are introduced to the Parliament, where they must pass through both houses by a simple majority. If they fail to pass both houses, committees from each chamber are created to reach a compromise. Failing that, the bill is returned to whoever wrote it. A bill that is passed by both chambers is delivered to the Cabinet and the president, who may sign the bill into law or return it for reconsideration, similar to the American presidential veto. If the latter happens, the bill is voted on again and must pass both chambers by a 2/3 majority to override the president. If the votes are in favor, the bill becomes law.

In addition to their interactions in the lawmaking process, the legislative and executive branches balance each other's power through a system of checks and balances. Each branch has the right to be informed of the other's agendas, and each is legally required to disclose important information. The executive officers may address the legislature when they wish and Parliament may conduct private or public commissions to investigate the actions of the president or Cabinet. Further, Parliament may force Cabinet members to resign through a vote of no confidence, and the president may dissolve the Chamber of Deputies once during each term of office.

The Judicial Branch

The power of the judicial branch of the government is vested in the Supreme Court and other courts established by the constitution. The judiciary is independent and separate from the legislative and executive branches. Except where provided by law, judges confirmed in office are appointed for life and cannot be removed.

The court levels are the Supreme Court, the High Court of the Republic, the Provincial Courts, the Court of the City of Kigali, the District Courts, and the Municipality and Town Courts. Currently, the country's specialized courts are the military courts and the *Gacaca*, which are the locally based tribunals established to help prosecute the tens of thousands of prisoners who await trial for genocide offenses.

A prisoner stands trial in a Gacaca or "grass" court, where villagers and judges convene to try those accused of genocide crimes. There are more than 11,000 Gacaca courts throughout Rwanda addressing genocide crimes.

The Supreme Court is the highest court in the country and is not subject to appeal except for special petitions for mercy or revision of decision. The Court's decisions are binding on all parties and it can try matters of high treason and criminal cases respecting members of high office.

Judges are appointed by the president, subject to the approval of an absolute majority of the Senate. The Senate also elects the two highest officers to the court, a president and a vice president, for a single term of eight years. These officers must be career judges and meet high professional, educational, and moral requirements as set out by the constitution.

Gacaca Courts

The Gacaca courts were established in 2001 by Rwandan law to relieve the burden on the national justice system. According to the Gacacas' proponents, the governing principle in all the cases is to bring together all of the protagonists at the actual location of the crime, including the survivors, witnesses, and alleged perpetrators. Prisoners who confess to their guilt are released to return to their village or city, where the local Gacaca pronounces its judgment.

The courts are governed by the 2001 Gacaca law, which assigns each accused genocide participant a category according to the severity of his or her offense. The categories range from Class 1 offenders, who planned and led the genocide, to Class 4 offenders, who committed minor property crimes.

From their inception the Gacaca courts have received criticism from human rights groups and legal organizations for several reasons, among which are that the judges are not adequately trained and the accused are not provided with legal counsel. In December 2003, independent legal organizations in Rwanda declared that the Gacaca practices violated the 2003 constitution and urged the government to reevaluate the courts.

Political Parties

At present, there are nine active political parties in Rwanda. The Party for Democratic Renewal, headed by former president Pasteur Bizimungu, is officially banned by the government, and Bizimungu is currently imprisoned on charges of threatening state security and illegal possession of a firearm.

Political parties were first formed in Rwanda in 1959 prior to the Hutu revolution. During the Habyarimana government (1974–94), all but the president's own National Movement for Democracy and Development (MRND) party were banned until 1992, at the end of the civil war. One of the conditions of the Arusha Accords, which declared the civil war over, was the legalization of multiple parties. Most of the parties in existence today were formed during this period.

In late 1994, all parties except the MRND were represented in a transitional multiparty National Assembly; however, the RPF held the majority of power. Early in 2002, under President Kagame the government banned all parties except the RPF from organizing until 2003. The government defended the ban by claiming it was a way to prevent ethnic divisions from forming within the parties. In April of that year, Pasteur Bizimungu and several others were imprisoned for political organizing and other charges.

The new Rwandan constitution, ratified in 2003, officially established the right of political parties to organize as long as they abided by the constitution,

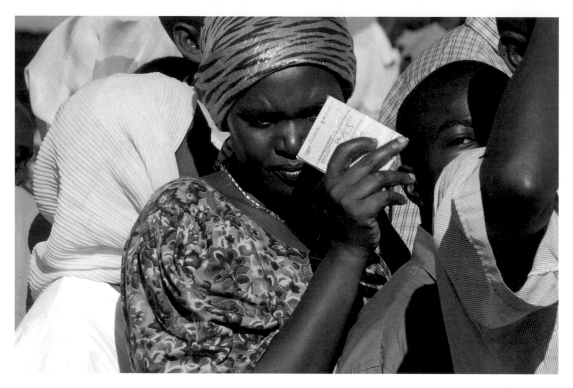

In May 2003, voters stand in line for the first multiparty election in Rwandan history. On the momentous day, crowds of Rwandans formed at voting polls all over the country.

followed a policy of non-discriminatory membership, and reflected national unity. These parties were also allowed to find representation in Parliament. However, despite the inclusiveness of the new constitution, human rights and political rights organizations have repeatedly accused Kagame and the RPF-dominated government of obstructing the free exercise of the parties by stifling opposition under the guise of protecting national unity.

Further restrictions on party affiliation are written into the new constitution. Those holding the country's two most powerful offices, president and Speaker of the Chamber of Deputies, are required to belong to different political parties. Additionally, judges, prosecutors, and members of the armed forces, police, and National Security Service are prohibited from belonging to political organizations. These restrictions are meant to prevent party or ethnic politics from gaining enough momentum to cause ethnic violence.

Voting

Under the Hutu government (1960s–early 1990s), voting in Rwanda was an empty gesture because there was only one party to choose. Today, the people's votes count for more. In August and December 2003, the country held its first multiparty presidential and parliamentary elections in history.

In both elections, the vast majority of the country's 4 million eligible voters turned out to cast their ballots all over the country. Polling places were overwhelmed, with long lines forming before dawn. Shops closed for the day and many people turned out in their most colorful, festive clothing. Because of the country's high illiteracy, the government made it easy to vote for those unable to read or write. Voters simply marked their thumbprint next to a large color photograph of their chosen candidate.

(Opposite) Three generations of Rwandan villagers share a laugh in a sorghum field. Sorghum and tea are important exports in the country's largely agricultural economy. (Right) A Hutu field worker proudly displays his fine tea harvest.

4 A Struggling Economy

RWANDA IS THE MOST densely populated country in Africa, is landlocked, possessing almost no navigable waterways for transportation or trade, and has few natural resources and minimal industry. It also has one of the world's poorest economies, appearing in 2003 on the United Nations' list of the 49 Least Developed Countries (LDC). Approximately 60 percent of the population lives below the poverty level, with 90 percent of the country's labor force working in agriculture on *subsistence-level farms*. The remaining 10 percent of the labor force has government and service jobs or works in Rwanda's struggling industries. Accurate unemployment figures for Rwanda are not available; however, unemployment is high throughout the country.

The severe damage caused by the 1994 genocide can explain many of Rwanda's current economic woes. The war impoverished the population and

45

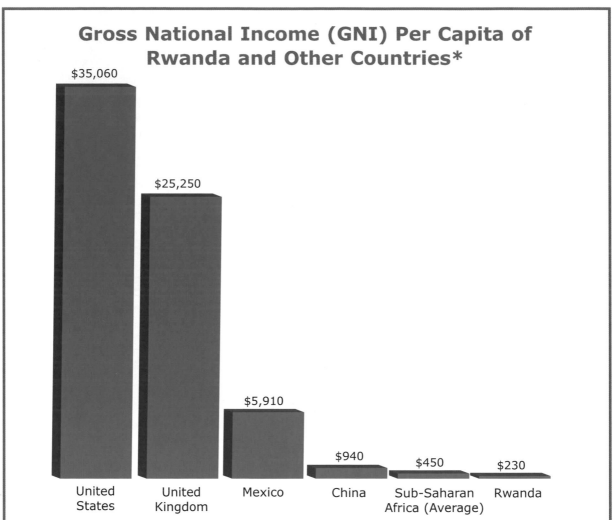

Gross National Income (GNI) Per Capita of Rwanda and Other Countries*

- United States — $35,060
- United Kingdom — $25,250
- Mexico — $5,910
- China — $940
- Sub-Saharan Africa (Average) — $450
- Rwanda — $230

*Gross national income per capita is the total value of all goods and services produced domestically in a year, supplemented by income received from abroad, divided by midyear population. The above figures take into account fluctuations in currency exchange rates and differences in inflation rates across global economies.

Figures are 2002 estimates. Source: World Bank, 2003.

made it difficult for businesses to attract investment. However, since 1996 Rwanda has made limited but steady progress in rehabilitating its economy.

Economic Sectors

Most of Rwanda's agriculture is produced on small farms scattered around the country. In addition to providing food for locals, 45 percent of the *gross national income (GNI)* comes from agriculture grown mostly on foreign-owned farms. These crops include coffee, tea, and pyrethrum, a flower used in the manufacture of insecticide. Major crops traditionally produced for local consumption are beans and peas, sweet potatoes, cassava, corn, sorghum, ground nuts, and millet and other cereal grains.

Several serious factors impede agricultural production: The country's mountainous terrain makes using machine-operated or even cattle-drawn farm equipment impractical. Thus, the planting, tending, and harvesting of crops must be performed by hand. In addition, extreme population density, many decades of poor farming practices, deforestation for wood fuel, and a climate producing seasons of hard rains and frequent drought have severely reduced the amount of arable land. Often, the levels of domestic food production are inadequate and additional food must be imported.

Rwanda's climate and sloped terrain in the western part of the country and the central plateaus are ideal for coffee and tea growth. During colonial rule, the Germans and then the Belgians forced Rwandan farmers to extensively plant coffee for export. Consequently, Rwanda became dependent on coffee as its major export, and the collapse of coffee prices in the late 1980s devastated the economy. In the late 1990s, coffee and tea plantations were rehabilitated and exports increased. Tea production reached over 14 million tons per year, making it Rwanda's largest export. Nevertheless, low prices of coffee and tea worldwide have slowed the country's recovery.

In recent years, the Rwandan government's attempts to diversify into alternative agriculture exports, such as flowers and vegetables, have been unsuccessful. A major obstacle facing this plan is the country's poor transportation system, which makes it difficult to deliver fresh goods abroad.

Industry and Service

Rwanda's manufacturing sector contributes approximately 20 percent of the *gross domestic product (GDP)*; however, almost none of the goods manufactured in the country are for export but instead are low-cost substitutes for items too expensive to import. These items include beer, soft drinks, cigarettes, soap, cement, textiles, plastic goods, and small agricultural tools such as hoes and wheelbarrows. Civil war and the genocide devastated the manufacturing industry, and it had to be rebuilt or repaired, mostly with foreign aid.

Domestic strife also severely damaged the retail trade, though it quickly revived following the return of Rwandan Tutsi refugees who opened new small businesses. Also, tourism has slowly picked up after dropping off considerably during the 1990s. However, poor infrastructure and continual safety concerns have kept the industry from flourishing.

Rwanda's telecommunications industry is becoming an increasingly important player in the Rwandan economy, though it is still in the developing stages. In 2002, there were approximately 600,000 telephone lines and more than 81,000 cell phones in use; however, much of the service was limited to the businesses and government facilities of Kigali.

The country has few televisions and no television broadcast stations. It has two Internet Service Providers but only approximately 20,000 users. The primary mode of communication is through three FM radio stations and one shortwave radio channel, all currently owned by the government.

Natural Resources and Energy

Rwanda's meager mineral resources account for about 5 percent of its foreign export earnings. These minerals are mostly heavy metals used in

Quick Facts: The Economy of Rwanda

Gross domestic product (GDP*): $8.92 billion

Inflation: 5.5%

Natural Resources: gold, cassiterite (tin ore), wolframite (tungsten ore), methane, hydropower, arable land

Agriculture (45% of GDP): coffee, tea, pyrethrum (insecticide made from chrysanthemums), bananas, beans, sorghum, potatoes; livestock

Industry (20% of GDP): cement, agricultural products, small-scale beverages, soap, furniture, shoes, plastic goods, textiles, cigarettes

Services (35% of GDP): government, other

Foreign Trade:
Exports–$68 billion: coffee, tea, hides, tin ore

Imports–$253 billion: foodstuffs, machinery and equipment, steel, petroleum products, cement and construction material

Economic Growth Rate: 9.7%

Currency Exchange Rate: U.S. $1 = 559.75 Rwandan francs (2004)

*GDP, or gross domestic product, is the total value of goods and services produced in a country annually.

All figures are 2002 estimates unless otherwise indicated.

Sources: CIA World Factbook, 2003; Bloomberg.com.

manufacturing, as well as small amounts of gold and sapphires.

The country's energy resources are limited as well, and it has to import almost one-third of its power from other countries. Almost all of the energy production is hydroelectric, created by Rwanda's numerous waterways. However, research indicates that the methane reserves beneath Lake Kivu could offer a much greater source of energy. The reserves, produced by lake bed bacteria, could potentially be converted into enough electricity to power the entire country for 400 years. However, there has not been enough financial investment in methane extraction to produce significant energy levels.

Aid and Investment

Since the late 1990s, Rwanda has been a recipient of economic aid and cautious foreign investment. This influx of money, along with the resettlement of displaced people and refugees, has greatly helped restabilize the economy. Production has increased to almost prewar levels, and inflation, which skyrocketed during the early and mid-1990s, has subsided.

In recent years, the government has distributed aid money into rebuilding its infrastructure and industry. Through cooperation with the International Monetary Fund and the World Bank, the government secured $810 million in debt relief from the organizations' Heavily Indebted Poor Country joint initiative in 2000. The package was approved for distribution in 2003, and there is hope that it will greatly improve the country's economy.

The government has been more than willing to play its own role in Rwanda's recovery. It has encouraged local and foreign investment by reducing tariffs, setting up financial and technical assistance, and promoting the country as an excellent opportunity for growth. Recently, foreign investment has been concentrated in the country's strongest industries—mining, tea and coffee, and tourism. Meanwhile, more attention is being given to small businesses, manufacturing, and other developing industries.

Despite these economic strategies and aid opportunities, numerous obstacles stand in the way of Rwanda's expansion. In addition to those already discussed, there is also the population's lack of education and training and high national defense expenditures (in 2002, Rwanda was rated to have the world's highest armed forces growth).

The government's long-term economic plans include aiming for consistent GDP growth, an increased rate of investment, and a reduction in the country's deficit through higher export revenue. By making these advances, Rwanda may rise from its status as a least-developed country, while also encouraging additional private and foreign investment.

A young mason worker helps build a wall for a new school in Kigali.

(Opposite) Two Intore dancers light the night sky with their bright costumes. The Intore, or "Chosen Ones," have been entertainers throughout history; centuries ago, they performed for the Royal Court. (Right) A Hutu handcrafts a decorative wooden item.

5 A Culture in Transition

EVEN AFTER THE 1994 genocide, which killed approximately 10 percent of the population, Rwanda remains Africa's most densely populated country in sub-Saharan Africa, at 590 people per square mile (230 per square kilometer).

Ninety-four percent of the population lives in rural regions, concentrated most heavily in places suitable for farming. Rwanda's urban residents live mostly in Kigali, or around administrative centers in the smaller towns and villages scattered throughout the country.

A Shared Culture

Almost every Rwandan belongs to the Hutu, Tutsi, or Twa. The three groups share a common language, the ancient Bantu dialect Kinyarwanda, as well as many of the same cultural traditions and religious beliefs. Prior to the

Quick Facts: The People of Rwanda

Population: 7,810,056
Ethnic Groups: Hutu 84%, Tutsi 15%, Twa (Pygmoid) 1%
Age structure:
0–14 years: 42.5%
15–64 years: 54.8%
65 years and over: 2.7%
Population growth rate: 1.84%
Birth rate: 40.1 births/1,000 population
Infant mortality rate: 102.61 deaths/1,000 live births
Death rate: 21.72 deaths/1,000 population
Life expectancy at birth:
total population: 39.33 years
male: 38.51 years
female: 40.18 years

Total fertility rate: 5.6 children born/woman
Religion: Roman Catholic 56.5%, Protestant 26%, Adventist 11.1%, Muslim 4.6%, indigenous beliefs 0.1%, none 1.7% (2001)
Languages: Kinyarwanda (official) universal Bantu vernacular, French (official), English (official), Kiswahili (Swahili) used in commercial centers
Literacy: 70.4%

All figures are 2003 estimates unless otherwise indicated.
Source: Adapted from CIA World Factbook, 2003.

1994 genocide, intermarriage between groups was not uncommon. Although ethnic tensions remain, the government is working hard to reintegrate the Rwandan people into a peaceful, multiethnic society.

The Hutu (also called Bahutu) are the largest ethnic group in Rwanda, making up approximately 84 percent of population. They are descendants of Bantu tribes who centuries ago lived in regions further to the north. The Tutsi (also called Watutsi or Batutsi) are the second most populous group and make up 15 percent of population. They descended from nomadic cattle herdsmen and warriors from the Nile River basin who came to the Rwandan region in search of land for cattle grazing.

The Twa (also called Batwa) are a Pygymy people who make up less than 1 percent of population. They are descendants from the first people to live in East-Central Africa, and in the past they preferred to live in the high-altitude forests. Over the centuries, as Hutus and Tutsis cleared trees to cultivate the land, the Twa moved deeper into the forests, while those who remained in or near Tutsi settlements often became dancers, jesters, and guards.

Today, deforestation has robbed the Twa of their habitat. They are the poorest group in Rwandan society, with virtually no representation in local or national government. Most of them lack formal education and skills; however, a few have learned to farm or to make a meager living by making pottery, doing odd jobs, and begging. In recent years, the Twa have organized and have applied pressure on the government to gain more political representation.

Refugees and Prisoners

Rwanda has a large refugee population, with 120.59 refugees for every 1,000 people. These refugees are Rwandan Hutus and Tutsis who have returned after fleeing civil violence and other groups who have sought refuge from violence occurring elsewhere.

Rwanda also has an alarming number of prisoners, many imprisoned for crimes committed during the 1994 genocide. Before legislation ordered the release of 40,000 of these prisoners in January 2003, there was a total of more than 115,000 of them. Many of the prisoners were arrested in the mid-late

Hutu refugees cross the border into Tanzania to escape the tribal violence, May 1994. During the civil war, both Tutsis and Hutus fled from the fighting and chaos. Many have since returned to rebuild their lives.

1990s (some were just children at the time) and have been languishing in overcrowded jails for nearly a decade without facing trial. The underfunded prisons have been plagued by disease, malnutrition, and violence.

In 2001, pressured by international human rights groups and other governments, Rwandan legislators enacted the Gacaca law, which allowed prisoners to be released and tried in their own villages. Those who were not released face a long wait for their trials.

Family Life

The most important unit in the Rwandan culture is the *inzu*, which in Kinyarwanda means "family or clan." It can also mean "household." The inzu is traditionally comprised of a father, mother, children, and relatives from the father's side.

Members of an inzu often live together on a rural homestead called a *rugo*, which is made up of several beehive-shaped houses, each woven from branches and thatch and covered with clay and cow dung for insulation. Additional houses are built as the family grows, and if the inzu is large, the family may live in adjoining rugos. However, the lack of available land often makes such traditional living arrangements difficult. While there are a few Western-style houses in urban areas, most Rwandans in cities and towns live in houses similar to those built in rural areas,

Home architectural styles in Rwanda vary greatly from urban areas to small villages like this one. Regardless of location, family remains paramount in Rwandan life.

except for the corrugated iron roofs that protect their homes.

Large families are common, and a family without children is considered incomplete. Kinship relationships still remain important in contemporary culture, but the *umuhana*, a close group of neighboring rugos, has gained importance as a social unit. Individuals in the *umuhana*, related or not, cooperate and support each other in farming, herding, and other social matters.

Every Rwandan is expected to marry. Only an estimated 5 percent of Rwandan women reach the age of 50 unwed. While some Rwandans find their mates on their own, many marriages are arranged by Rwandan fathers. According to tradition, if a Rwandan man wants to marry a woman not chosen for him, he must have his father's approval.

Before a marriage can take place, the groom's family must pay the bride's family a dowry, often consisting of livestock or farm tools. In recent years, Rwandans have married later in life because they can't meet the dowry's expenses or find an available plot on which to set up a new household.

On the day of a wedding, called the *bukwe*, the wedding procession walks from the groom's house with gifts and the dowry and delivers them to the bride's house. Tradition dictates that the bride resist leaving her home and family until the groom presents her with gifts, at which point she then joins the procession. At the *kurongora* or wedding ceremony, the bride is crowned with flowers and introduced to the groom's family, which welcomes her as its own. A celebratory feast with drink, song, and dance follows, after which the groom takes his bride to his family's rugo.

Most children are born at home with the help of a midwife and neighbors. Six days after the child is born, neighbors bring gifts. In keeping with a practice of keeping away evil spirits, parents bury the placenta under the bed and rub the infant with butter every day for six months. Because of Rwanda's high infant mortality rate, parents wait several months to name their children, at which point their survival is more assured. Typically, Rwandan fathers choose their children's names, which reflect their heritage and the family's hopes for their future.

Divorce in Rwanda is common and easy to obtain. Marriage can be terminated with *gutana*, a simple ritual in which a husband sends his wife back

While indigenous beliefs have survived in Rwanda, Christianity is the most popular religion, followed by Islam. Catholic cathedrals like this famous one in Butare can be found all over the country.

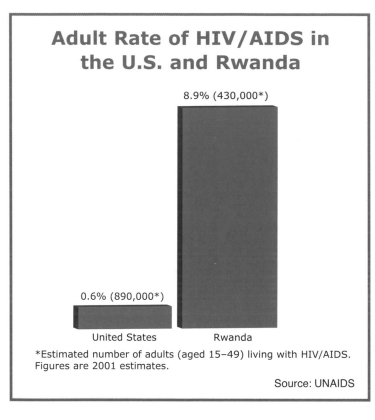

Adult Rate of HIV/AIDS in the U.S. and Rwanda

8.9% (430,000*)

0.6% (890,000*)

United States   Rwanda

*Estimated number of adults (aged 15–49) living with HIV/AIDS. Figures are 2001 estimates.

Source: UNAIDS

to her family or she leaves of her own accord. The wife's family will attempt to reconcile the couple, but if that does not occur, the wedding dowry must be returned to the husband's family. At that point, the divorce is final.

When an individual dies, everyone in the family participates in funeral rites, called *urupfu*. They halt all their work, and as they prepare for the funeral, neighbors are expected to help with any tasks that need to be done. The deceased's body is rubbed with butter and put in a crouching position with its arms and legs bound together to prevent the person's spirit from re-entering the body. The family then buries the body on its rugo, near a specially constructed spirit house where ancestral spirits are believed to dwell.

These observances reflect how indigenous beliefs have survived over time, in spite of the growing influence of Christianity and Islam. The core activity of traditional religions is the worship of a supreme being called Imana, who can only be addressed through the spirits of deceased family members or revered ancient spirits named Ryangombe and Nyabingi. Most Rwandans are Roman Catholic, though nearly all meld traditional practices with the sacraments of the Church. Protestant Rwandans are fewer in number, and there is an even smaller segment of Muslims.

Education and Health Care

The Rwandan school system follows the Western approach, which has survived from the mission schools founded by the Germans and the Belgians. Over half of Rwanda's population is literate, but few people have received education beyond primary school.

The Rwandan government wants to achieve universal primary education for all citizens by 2010 and has made efforts to increase the availability of secondary school, university, and technical training. However, dropout rates are high for primary school, and few Rwandans can afford higher education.

Rwanda's health care facilities are more advanced than those of many neighboring African countries, yet a lack of trained personnel has resulted in limited staff numbers. Also, because the health care system is fee-based, few Rwandans can afford medical assistance. International humanitarian organizations such as Doctors Without Borders provide a good deal of service, but these efforts have not been enough to stem Rwanda's health care crisis. Life expectancy figures for Rwandans are lower than the African average and have worsened since the 1994 genocide.

Currently, the health care system is most concerned with maintaining controls on fertility and disease. Malnutrition, malaria, and HIV/AIDS are the most serious threats to the population. In 1998, roughly 50 percent of all deaths in hospitals were caused by malaria, and in 2002, 13.7 percent of the adult population was infected with AIDS.

The Arts

Very little literature has been written in Rwanda's native language, Kinyarwanda, but a number of native authors have written books in French. The predominate Kinyarwandan literary forms remain unwritten. Rwanda's rich oral tradition has been expressed through epic poetry, public speaking, and storytelling, all forms that have helped celebrate, chronicle, and preserve history and myths through the generations.

Rwandan literature was once divided into two types: royal literature, which was sanctioned by the king and court, and popular literature, which was not. Royal literature included poetry, explanations of rituals, royal mythology, and long, intricate genealogies. Popular literature included military hymns and music, proverbs and sayings, and heroic poetry celebrating the ancestors of the Tutsi, Hutu, and Twa.

Today, storytelling and public speaking are still honored skills, and good storytellers are admired and welcomed into homes. All family members will gather to listen to a dramatic telling of a story. Many stories are instructive with a clear moral, while others detail the exploits of heroes or the types of suffering that evil spirits inflict. In payment for their service, storytellers often receive a meal or a small gift from a family.

In the handicraft field, Rwandans produce numerous useful and beautiful handmade objects. Women weave mats, baskets, and pot holders made from banana leaves, grasses, and fibers. Men make drums, pipes, bowls, jugs,

The Twa, who were the original inhabitants of Rwanda, are known for their skills as potters. Many have been displaced from their forest homes and have had to panhandle or find various forms of manual labor.

and other useful and decorative items out of wood. Additionally, both men and women use cow dung to create abstract paintings. These pictures are dominated by black, brown, and white geometric shapes and spirals.

Music and dance also have an important place in Rwanda's ethnic heritage. Nearly every celebration is accompanied by music and dancing.

Colorful handmade fabrics and fresh fruits brighten this outdoor market.

Drums are popular for religious rites, celebrations, and dances, and orchestras of seven to nine drummers bring together distinct tones to produce complex rhythms. Other traditional Rwandan instruments include the *lulunga*, an eight-stringed harp-like instrument played alone or accompanying a singer, a thumb piano called the *kalimba*, and various flutes made from reeds.

During the reign of the Tutsi kingdom, the royal court was entertained by Tutsi dancers known as the Intore, which means "the chosen ones." The male dancers were male warriors whose dance depicted combat, while the female dancers used graceful dance styles that bore comparisons to ballet. These and other forms of traditional dance are featured in Rwanda's national ballet, which is one of the country's most valued cultural treasures.

In addition to time-honored musical styles, contemporary music is also popular in Rwanda. Most people have access to a radio, over which the national station plays American rock and other popular music from around the world.

Sports and Recreation

Competitive running, high jumping, and wrestling are popular sports for Rwandans from a young age; however, soccer is the country's favorite. Both men and children enjoy playing informal soccer games, and if fans cannot attend professional matches, they listen to the games on the radio. In recent years, adult women have played for clubs in Kigali. The Rwandan national soccer team, which in 2004 qualified for the widely followed Africa Cup of Nations tournament, has become one of Rwanda's most unifying forces. Hutu and Tutsi fans will come together to celebrate the team's victories.

Watching films and television is rare in Rwanda, particularly outside Kigali. Many people instead entertain themselves with games. Children enjoy conventional favorites such as hide and seek, skipping, and hopscotch, and both children and adults play traditional board games.

(Opposite) Kigali City, the capital of Rwanda, is the largest urban area in the country and the most Westernized. Most tourists stay here when they visit, taking advantage of the city's modern facilities. (Right) Outside of Rwanda's large cities, typical homes are modest and often lack basic technology.

6 Cities, Towns, and Villages

RWANDA IS DIVIDED into 12 provinces called *intaras*. Each of these provinces is subdivided into districts called *akareres* and municipalities called *umujyis*. Other than Kigali City, the provinces are mostly rural, with a majority of residents living in arable areas. Although Rwanda is densely populated, only approximately 6 percent of Rwandans lives in urban areas and only three cities—Kigali City, Ruhengeri, and Butare—have more than 30,000 residents.

Rural regions are extremely overcrowded, owing to the large migration of Rwandan refugees and released prisoners who have returned from neighboring countries. Refugees and prisoners have returned to find their homes and land taken over by others. The situation has left many homeless, living wherever they can find space, beneath shelters of plastic sheeting.

Many of these individuals were participants in the 1994 genocide who have returned to live side by side with the families of the slaughtered. Rwanda's cities are experiencing a similar problem with the migration, but with no available land and few employment opportunities, the population growth has been lower in urban areas than in the countryside.

The National University of Rwanda seeks to help rebuild a skilled workforce, and students are eager to participate. The tiny campus now holds almost three times more students than its normal capacity.

Kigali City

Rwanda's capital city is also the largest city. With a population of approximately 305,700 in 2004, Kigali is at least seven times more populous than any other city in the country. Founded in 1907 under German colonial rule, the city became the capital in 1962, when Rwanda gained independence from Belgium.

Located in the central plateau region near the country's center, Kigali is Rwanda's main administrative and economic center, with an international airport and road access to all of the country's borders. The city is renowned for its wide variety of colorful plants and flowers and its appealing views of the outlying rolling hills. It is also the site of the National Library.

Kigali is also the most Westernized of Rwanda's urban areas. Much of the *expatriate* community lives there, and telephones, cell phones, Internet access, and other modern communications are available to residents. Numerous bars, nightclubs, and restaurants line the streets, serving a wide variety of European ethnic cuisine in addition to African fare. Many Kigali residents have government office jobs or work in the business sector. Nearby, iron ore is mined and the city has a large iron smelting plant, built in the 1980s.

The people of Kigali are still haunted by memories of the thousands of Tutsis slaughtered in the genocide, as well as the widespread and fierce fighting between the army and the Rwandan Patriotic Front (RPF) in 1990. During those years, a good portion of the infrastructure was damaged or destroyed and is still being rebuilt. The nearby villages of Nyamata and Ntarama suffered some of the worst genocidal violence. The bones of many victims still lie in plain sight, their bodies often left where they fell as memorials.

Ruhengeri

With a population of approximately 40,900 people in 2004, Ruhengeri is the second-largest city in Rwanda. Like many of the smaller towns and villages around Rwanda, the city was an independent state until the 20th century, when the Tutsi king annexed it with the help of colonial rulers. The date of Ruhengeri's founding is not known, though it is estimated that the city was settled sometime in the 17th century.

Situated at the base of the Virunga Mountains, approximately 60 miles (100 km) northwest of Kigali, Ruhengeri is a popular destination for wildlife enthusiasts who wish to see the mountain gorillas of Volcanoes National Park. The park was closed for several years during the mid-1990s because of fighting, and it remained closed between 1994 to 1999 because of Hutu militia activity and unexploded ordnance.

Butare

Butare is Rwanda's third-largest city with a population of approximately 39,600 people in 2004. Located in the southcentral region of the country, the town is about 20 miles (30 km) from the Burundi border. Butare was founded in 1920 as the capital city of the former Ruanda-Urundi territory. (At that time it was named Astrida after Astrid, the queen of Belgium.) It was the largest and most important city in Rwanda prior to independence, when it lost its bid to become the new nation's capital.

Although it is much smaller than Kigali and Ruhengeri, Butare has the reputation of being the country's intellectual and cultural center because of its numerous attractions. It has the National Institute of Scientific Research, the National Museum, and one of two branches of the Rwandan National University. The National Institute of Scientific Research maintains three specialized research centers: one devoted to pharmacology (the study of drugs), another to energy, and another to Rwandan studies. The National Museum, which ranks among the best in eastern Africa, houses archaeological and ethnographic displays as well as a photograph collection documenting Rwanda's history from precolonial times.

Situated near Butare is the village of Nyabisindu, formerly Nyanza, which was the historic seat of Rwanda's feudal monarchy. The Royal Palace at Nyanza, a large domed construction of traditional materials, stands today as a relic of the period. Another attraction outside Butare is Gihindamuyaga, a village drawing tourists for its handicrafts, goldsmithing, and jam factory.

Gisenyi

With a population of 30,300 in 2004, Gisenyi is the fourth-largest town in Rwanda. It is located in the west, on the northeastern shore of Lake Kivu and the border with the Democratic Republic of Congo.

Gisenyi is divided into two sections, consisting of one busy center with a small market area, and another quieter district with banks, government buildings, old colonial homes, and hotels. The town's waterfront features red sandy beaches offering swimming, sunbathing, and water sports as well as numerous upscale hotels. Due to its natural beauty and attractiveness,

The Royal Palace at Nyanza, made completely of natural materials, was once home to the feudal monarchy. It has been fully restored and now serves as a museum.

Gisenyi is one of the more expensive towns in Rwanda and a popular destination for Rwanda's wealthier class of expatriates and travelers. During the colonial days under Belgium, a large number of wealthy European colonists and Tutsi aristocrats lived in this area. Away from the resorts, the Lake Kivu area offers a glimpse into traditional African life. Fishermen on the lake use dugout wooden canoes whose design has not changed for centuries.

Along with being a tourist attraction, Gisenyi also has a darker side. During the era of the Hutu Republic, it became one of the most conservative anti-Tutsi towns. The greater Gisenyi area was the site of some of the swiftest genocidal violence against the Tutsis and moderate Hutus, and it was one of the last places where the Hutu extremist government held out against the RPF before fleeing into Zaire (Democratic Republic of Congo) in July 1994.

A Calendar of Rwandan Festivals

January

New Year's Day is observed with both reflection and celebration. People typically gather for speeches, traditional dances, and feasts.

July

Two important national holidays occur in the first week of July. On July 1, Rwandans celebrate **Independence Day** to remember the end of Belgian colonial rule (1962); on July 4, they celebrate **National Liberation Day**, which marks the Rwandan Patriotic Front's capture of the capital and the end of the genocide in 1994. Rwandans observe the holidays with a weeklong festival that features dancing, speeches, feasting, and a widely attended soccer match.

Also taking place in July is a celebration honoring **Ryangombe**, Rwanda's most powerful ancestral spirit. Members of the religious fraternity called the *babandwa* celebrate by painting their bodies and decorating huts.

August

A ritual called **Umuganura** is observed in August to mark the harvest. The deity Imana is believed to reside over the first harvest, and celebrations include a festive meal and the drinking of sorghum beer with family and friends.

On August 15, Rwandan Christians celebrate **Assumption Day**, marking the Virgin Mary's ascent into heaven after the death of Jesus. They usually attend church and have a special family meal.

November

On November 1, Rwandan Christians celebrate **All Saints' Day**, honoring those who have achieved sainthood as well as the dead.

December

Christmas is celebrated by Rwandan Christians on December 25 with a church service, a special family meal, and sometimes the exchange of gifts.

Religious Observances

Rwandan Muslims and Christians observe a number of important holy days related to their religions. Some of these are on particular days each year (for example, **Christmas**, which is observed on December 25, is the Christian celebration of the birth of Jesus). However, many other major celebrations are held according to a lunar calendar, in which the months are related to the phases of the moon. A lunar month is shorter than the typical month of the Western calendar. Therefore, the festival dates vary from year to year. Other celebrations are observed seasonally.

A very important month of the Muslim lunar calendar is the ninth month, **Ramadan**. This is a time of sacrifice for devout Muslims. Rwandan Muslims celebrate **Eid al-Fitr** to mark the end of Ramadan. **Eid al-Adha** (Feast of Sacrifice) takes place in the last month of the Muslim calendar during the hajj period, when Muslims make a pilgrimage to Mecca. The holiday honors the prophet Abraham, who was willing to sacrifice his own son to Allah. Each of these holidays is celebrated with a feast. On Eid al-Adha, families traditionally eat a third of the feast and donate the rest to the poor.

The major Christian festivals on the lunar cycle involve the suffering and death of Jesus Christ. **Ash Wednesday** marks the start of a period of self-sacrifice called **Lent**, which lasts for 40 days. The final eight days of Lent are known as Holy Week. A number of important days are observed, including **Palm Sunday**, which commemorates Jesus' arrival in Jerusalem; **Holy Thursday**, which marks the night of the Last Supper; **Good Friday**, the day of Jesus' death on the cross; and **Easter Monday**, which marks his resurrection. (In Western countries, Easter is typically celebrated on the day before.)

Recipes

Rwandan Chicken

(Serves 4)
1 chicken, cut into pieces
3 Tbsp. oil
1 onion, thinly sliced
3 large tomatoes, mashed
2 stalks of celery, cut into thin rounds
1 tsp. salt
1 hot pimento or chili pepper

Directions:
1. Fry the chicken in hot oil until golden.
2. Remove pieces and cook onions in the same pot. When they are golden brown, return chicken pieces to the pot and add tomatoes, celery, salt, and hot pepper.
3. Reduce heat and simmer. Serve when chicken is tender.

Banana Fritters

1 cup all-purpose flour
2 Tbsp. sugar
2 tsp. baking powder
1/4 tsp. salt
1 large plantain
1/2 cup milk
1 egg
1 Tbsp. cooking oil

Directions:
1. In a mixing bowl, stir together flour, sugar, baking powder, and salt. Set aside.
2. Peel banana and slice into two-inch chunks.
3. In a blender container, combine banana, milk, egg, and cooking oil.
4. Cover and blend until smooth.
5. Add egg mixture to the dry ingredients and blend.
6. Heat oil to 375ºF.
7. Carefully drop one rounded teaspoon of mixture into deep oil and fry fritters, a few at a time, for 2 1/2 to 3 minutes or until done, turning once.
8. Drain on paper towel. Serve warm with powdered sugar if desired.

Peanuts-Nougat

1 lb. peeled roasted peanuts, crushed ground
1 1/2 cups of sugar
Lemon juice

Directions:
1. Melt sugar and lemon juice in a pan.
2. When sugar gets brown, add peanuts and stir with a wooden spoon.
3. Pour nougat on a greased pan and roll out to a thickness of a quarter-inch.
4. Cut into 2-inch squares and serve.

Isombe

2 bunches cassava leaves, washed and chopped (another leafy vegetable may be substituted)
2 green onions, chopped
2 medium eggplants, cut into chunks
2 packages spinach, washed and chopped
2 green peppers, sliced into pieces
3 Tbsp. palm oil
3 Tbsp. peanut butter

Directions:
1. Boil cassava leaves until tender.
2. Add chopped green onions, eggplant, spinach, and green peppers.
3. Cook on medium heat for 10 minutes.
4. Add palm oil and peanut butter.
5. Simmer for 10 minutes, stirring occasionally. Serve with rice or bread.

Pinto Beans with Potatoes

(Serves 6 to 8)
2 cups dried pinto beans, presoaked
3 large potatoes, chopped
2 celery stalks, chopped
1 tsp. salt
1 onion, thinly sliced
4 Tbsp. peanut oil

Directions:
1. Cover the pinto beans with water, bring to a boil, then reduce heat and simmer until beans are just tender.
2. Add the potato chunks, celery and salt, along with more water if necessary to cover. Continue to cook over low heat.
3. Just before the potatoes and beans are tender, gently fry the onion in a large, heavy skillet or stew pot.
4. Using a slotted spoon, add the beans and potatoes to the pot, and stir until well mixed and heated through.
5. Serve hot over rice or a stiff porridge.

Reprinted from *The Africa News Cookbook: African Cooking for Western Kitchens*, edited by Tami Hultman. New York: Penguin, 1985.

Glossary

annexed—incorporated into an existing political unit such as a country, state, county, or city.

apartheid—a policy or practice of segregating groups of people.

bicameral—containing two chambers.

cash crop—a crop grown for direct sale.

clemency—mercy or pardon given for a crime.

deforestation—the removal of trees from an area of land.

drought—a long period of abnormally low rainfall that adversely affects agriculture or living conditions.

expatriate—one who has taken up residence in a foreign land.

feudal—having the characteristics of an old political and economic system in Europe involving a power relationship between landowner (lord) and borrower (vassal).

Gacaca—local tribunals in Rwanda established to put genocide participants before trial.

gross domestic product (GDP)—the total value of goods and services produced within a country in a year.

gross national income (GNI)—the total value of all goods and services produced domestically in a year, supplemented by income from abroad.

manifesto—a public declaration of principles, policies, or intentions, especially of a political nature.

methane—a flammable gas used as a fuel, known by the symbol CH4.

promulgate—to put into effect by formal public announcement.

propaganda—the spreading of ideas that reflect the views and interests of those advocating it.

referendum—direct popular vote on a proposed public measure or statute.

savanna—a flat lowland of tropical or subtropical regions.

sovereign—self-governing or independent.

subsistence-level farming—a farming level in which the produce is barely sufficient to feed the people who grow it.

tectonic—relating to the rock structures and external forms resulting from the deformation of the earth's crust.

tributary—a stream that flows into a larger stream or other body of water.

watershed—a ridge of high land dividing two areas that are drained by different river systems.

Project and Report Ideas

Report Ideas

With the help of a teacher or librarian, find the current population information about Rwanda. (You can also find this data on the CIA World Fact Book website at http://www.cia.gov/cia/publications/factbook/geos/rw.html.) Using this information, answer the questions below:

1. How many people were born and how many died in Rwanda this year?
2. How much did the population increase? What percentage growth does that number represent?
3. How large is Rwanda in square miles and square kilometers?
4. Approximately how many people are there per square mile and square kilometer?

Now find out the same information for your state and compare it with the Rwandan information. Based on these comparisons, discuss what you think your state would be like if it had the same population density that Rwanda does.

Using this book and research material from the library or Internet, write a one-page report on the history of the Tutsi kingdom in Rwanda. In your report, discuss the class structure of the Tutsis, Hutus, and Twa under the kingdom. How did that relationship change when Rwanda was colonized by Germany and then Belgium? Do you think the conditions in Rwanda would be different if the country had not been colonized? If so, how?

Presentation Ideas

With assistance from a teacher, parent, or librarian, use the library or Internet to find out how many Rwandan Francs were exchanged for a U.S. dollar in 1994. Then find out how many Rwandan Francs are exchanged for a dollar today. What percentage difference is there between the two figures? Present an oral presentation that gives some of the reasons why the value has changed so much.

Research the mountain gorilla. You may want to read about expert Dian Fossey and her work with the gorillas in Rwanda. Prepare a short presentation for your class on this species. In your report, describe the mountain gorilla in detail, touching on its appearance, behavior, and habitat.

Use the library or Internet to learn about explorers John Hanning Speke and Richard Burton. Prepare a short oral presentation for your class on their contributions to the exploration of East Africa and the history of Rwanda.

Find out more about African drums, the *lulunga*, the *kalimba*, or any other traditional Rwandan instrument. Find out how it is made and what materials are used. If possible, find a picture of the instrument, a recording of it being played, or even the real instrument itself! Give an oral presentation on what you have learned.

Map

Using maps of Rwanda and information from this book, plan a railroad route connecting Kigali with other towns and villages. Use available information on elevation and terrain from the map to help plan the most level and efficient route. Keep in mind the potential problems and challenges a real-life engineer or planner would have. (For example, engineers can only use a limited amount of railroad track in their designs.) Draw your route and show it to your classmates, explaining why you chose the route you did.

Creative Projects

Rwanda's oral tradition includes stories and poetry describing historic events, heroes, and myths. In this tradition, create your own poem or short story about yourself, a hero you admire, or an important event in your family history. Is there a moral to the story? If so, what is it? Read your work with your family and your classmates.

Create a craft using natural materials from your area of the country. Weave a mat or a basket or create a collage.

Chronology

A.D. 600s–900s	Hutus migrate into land that is now Rwanda, already inhabited by the Twa.
1300–1400s	Tutsis migrate into Rwanda.
1600s–1800s	The Tutsi kingdom is established and becomes centralized.
1890	Along with neighboring Burundi, Rwanda becomes part of the German colony called German East Africa.
1923	Ruanda-Urundi (Rwanda-Burundi) becomes a Belgian colony, granted as a spoil of war by the League of Nations.
1959	The Hutus initiate a revolution against the Tutsi power structure.
1961	Rwanda is proclaimed a republic.
1962	Rwanda becomes independent with Gregoire Kayibanda, a Hutu, as Rwanda's president; many Tutsis flee the country to escape Hutu attacks.
1973	President Gregoire Kayibanda is ousted in a bloodless military coup led by Juvenal Habyarimana.
1978	A new constitution is ratified; Habyarimana is elected president.
1990	The Rwandan Patriotic Front (RPF) invades Rwanda from Uganda, starting a civil war.
1991	A new multiparty constitution is promulgated.
1993	President Habyarimana signs a power-sharing agreement with the Tutsis; a UN mission is sent to Rwanda monitor the peace agreement.

1994   On April 6, Habyarimana and the Burundian president Cyprien Ntaryamira are killed when their plane is shot down; genocidal violence against the Tutsis begins; between April and July, 800,000 Tutsis and moderate Hutus are killed; Hutu militias flee the country along with around 2 million Hutu refugees; in July, RPF forces finally take Kigali and Pasteur Bizimungu, a moderate Hutu, is announced the new president.

1995   The Rwandan government and the United Nations International Tribunal for Rwanda begin prosecuting genocide suspects; massive arrests are made in Rwanda, overcrowding prisons.

1996–2002   Thousands of Rwandan forces fight in Zaire/Democratic Republic of the Congo.

2000   In April, Bizimungu resigns and is replaced by Paul Kagame.

2001   In October, Gacaca judges are elected to preside over local community-based genocide tribunals; in December, the new Rwandan flag and national anthem are unveiled as symbols of national unity.

2003   In May, voters back new constitution designed to deter ethnic violence; in August, Paul Kagame wins landslide election victory; Rwanda's first multiparty elections take place in October and the Rwandan Patriotic Front party wins absolute majority.

2004   In keeping with the 2003 constitution, Rwandan leaders initiate campaign to root out corruption in government.

2005   On March 10, after more than three years, the first proper trials in Rwanda's Gacaca courts began.

Further Reading/Internet Resources

Carr, Rosamond Halsey with Ann Howard Halsey. *Land of a Thousand Hills: My Life in Rwanda.* New York: Viking, 1999.

Gourevitch, Philip. *We Wish to Inform You That Tomorrow We Will Be Killed with Our Families: Stories from Rwanda.* New York: Farrar, Strauss & Giroux, 1998.

Murphy, Dervla. *Visiting Rwanda.* Dublin, Ireland: Lilliput Press, 1998.

Neuffer, Elizabeth. *The Key to My Neighbor's House.* New York: Picador, 2001.

Peterson, Scott. *Me Against My Brother.* New York: Routledge, 2000.

Travel Information

http://www.lonelyplanet.com/destinations/africa/rwanda

History and Geography

http://www.worldatlas.com/webimage/countrys/africa/rw.htm
http://www.cyberschoolbus.un.org/infonation/index.asp

Economic and Political Information

http://www.ictr.org
http://news.bbc.co.uk/1/hi/world/africa/1288230.stm

Culture and Arts

http://www.rwanda-online.org/rwanda/online/Rwanda/Art%20and%20Culture
http://www.rwandatourism.com/culture.htm

Embassy of The Republic of Rwanda
1714 New Hampshire Avenue, NW
Washington, D.C. 20009
United States
202-232-2882/3/4

U.S. Embassy in Kigali, Rwanda
Information Resource Center (IRC)
Avenue de la Révolution
P.O. Box 28 Kigali
Rwanda
(250) 505601/02/03
KigaliEmbassy@state.gov

Index

Numbers in ***bold italic*** refer to captions.

Contributors/Picture Credits

Professor Robert I. Rotberg is Director of the Program on Intrastate Conflict and Conflict Resolution at the Kennedy School, Harvard University, and President of the World Peace Foundation. He is the author of a number of books and articles on Africa, including *A Political History of Tropical Africa* and *Ending Autocracy, Enabling Democracy: The Tribulations of Southern Africa*.

Andy Koopmans is the author of several other young adult books, including biographies, histories, and literary companions. He is also a published poet, essayist, and fiction writer. He lives in Seattle, Washington, with his wife, Angela Mihm, and their pets, Zachary, Bubz, and Licorice.